D1191921

CELEBRATING OUR HOLIDAYS

Celebrating
DIWALI

By Elizabeth Morgan and
Michelle Parker-Rock

Cavendish Square

New York

Published in 2023 by Cavendish Square Publishing, LLC
29 E. 21st Street New York, NY 10010

Copyright © 2023 by Cavendish Square Publishing, LLC

No part of this publication may be reproduced, stored in a retrieval system, or transmitted in any form or by any means—electronic, mechanical, photocopying, recording, or otherwise—without the prior permission of the copyright owner. Request for permission should be addressed to Permissions, Cavendish Square Publishing, 29 E. 21st Street New York, NY 10010. Tel (877) 980-4450; fax (877) 980-4454.

Website: cavendishsq.com

This publication represents the opinions and views of the author based on their personal experience, knowledge, and research. The information in this book serves as a general guide only. The author and publisher have used their best efforts in preparing this book and disclaim liability rising directly or indirectly from the use and application of this book.

Disclaimer: Portions of this work were originally authored by Michelle Parker-Rock and published as *Diwali: The Hindu Festival of Lights, Feasts, and Family*. All new material this edition authored by Elizabeth Morgan.

All websites were available and accurate when this book was sent to press.

Library of Congress Cataloging-in-Publication Data

Names: Morgan, Elizabeth, 1993- author. | Parker-Rock, Michelle, author.
Title: Celebrating Diwali / Elizabeth Morgan, Michelle Parker-Rock.
Description: New York : Cavendish Square Publishing, [2023] | Series:
Celebrating Our Holidays | Includes index.
Identifiers: LCCN 2021043810 | ISBN 9781502664976 (Set) | ISBN
9781502664983 (Library Binding) | ISBN 9781502664969 (Paperback) | ISBN
9781502664990 (eBook)
Subjects: LCSH: Divali–Juvenile literature.
Classification: LCC BL1239.82.D58 M675 2023 | DDC
394.265/45–dc23/eng/20211008
LC record available at https://lccn.loc.gov/2021043810

Editor: Katie Kawa
Copyeditor: Jill Keppeler
Designer: Deanna Paternostro

The photographs in this book are used by permission and through the courtesy of: Cover, p. 1 Mukesh Kumar/Shutterstock.com; back cover, pp. 3, 5, 6, 9, 11, 13, 15, 19, 21, 23, 25, 28, 29, 30, 31, 32 N.D.Vector/Shutterstock.com; pp. 4, 18 StockImageFactory.com/Shutterstock.com; p. 7 Creative Minds2/Shutterstock.com; p. 8 Prince9/Shutterstock.com; p. 10 reddees/Shutterstock.com; p. 11 Abie Davies/Shutterstock.com; p. 12 Irina Thalhammer/Shutterstock.com; p. 14 Dipak Shelare/Shutterstock.com; p. 16 StanislavBeloglazov/Shutterstock.com; p. 20 Kiran Joshi/Shutterstock.com; p. 21 Arisha Ray Singh/Shutterstock.com; p. 22 Hit1912/Shutterstock.com; p. 24 CRS PHOTO/Shutterstock.com; pp. 26-27 Snehal Jeevan Pailkar/Shutterstock.com; p. 28 India Picture/Shutterstock.com.

Some of the images in this book illustrate individuals who are models. The depictions do not imply actual situations or events.

CPSIA compliance information: Batch #CSCSQ23: For further information contact Cavendish Square Publishing LLC, New York, New York, at 1-877-980-4450.

Printed in the United States of America

Find us on

CONTENTS

Diwali is a celebration of light, and the celebrations often last for five days.

CHAPTER ONE
A Festival of Lights

Many different groups of people have holidays that celebrate the victory of light over darkness. For example, the Jewish people celebrate Hanukkah every winter. They think of it as a festival, or celebration, of lights. Another popular festival of lights is Diwali. It's known mainly as a Hindu holiday, but it's also celebrated by people who follow the belief systems of Jainism and Sikhism. There are many stories and **traditions** connected to this festival of lights, and they reach back thousands of years.

Roots in Ancient India

Celebrations of Diwali are held around the world today, but they began in India. It's hard to know exactly when and how people began celebrating this holiday because it has its roots in ancient times. However, people can use ancient texts, or writings, to find clues to how this festival took shape.

Many people believe Diwali grew out of ancient Indian harvest festivals. It's celebrated in late October or November, which is often considered harvest time—the time when crops are picked to be eaten or sold. For this reason—and others—Diwali is often connected to the Hindu goddess Lakshmi. She's the goddess of prosperity, or success, and Diwali may have started as a way to celebrate a successful harvest.

Celebrating Many Things

For some people in India, Diwali honors the marriage of Lakshmi and Vishnu—one of the main gods in the Hindu religion, or belief system. Some people honor other gods and goddesses during this holiday. Some also see it as the start of a new year.

For those who practice Jainism, the holiday honors an important holy figure known as Mahavira. During Diwali, Sikhs remember the return of an important leader after his time in captivity. Some people who practice Buddhism also celebrate Diwali.

This holiday means different things to different people. This is especially true because celebrations of Diwali have now spread from India and can be seen around the world, including in the United States. No two families celebrate it in exactly the same way. However, one of the most common stories told to celebrate Diwali is the story of Rama—a king and Hindu deity, or god.

Studying Sanskrit

The name Diwali comes from the word *dipavali*, which means "row of lights" in Sanskrit. This language is very important to the people of India. It's an ancient Asian language and is the formal language of the Hindu religion. While few Indians speak this language today, it's the root of many commonly spoken Indian languages. It's also the language used to describe celebrations of Diwali in ancient texts.

Many people from India have moved to different parts of the world. They've brought their traditions, including their Diwali traditions, with them. Respecting someone's holiday traditions—even if they're different from yours—is a great way to show you care about them and to make them feel welcome.

Rama—who's sometimes known as Lord Rama—
was believed to be an avatar, or earthly form,
of the god Vishnu. He's even considered the
most important god for some Hindus.

CHAPTER TWO
The Royal Tale of Rama

Most holidays have stories behind them, and Diwali is no different. Many Indians connect the holiday to the tale of an ancient leader and god named Rama. His return to his kingdom after many years filled with struggles was seen as a victory of good over evil—and light over darkness. Learning more about this story can help us see how it's reflected in some of today's Diwali traditions.

A Royal Wedding

The most popular story about Rama is known as *Ramayana*. This story begins with Rama's birth in India. He had dark skin, dark eyes, and black, curly hair. Rama was the heir to the kingdom of Ayodhya, and he was a human form of the god Vishnu. Rama was strong, handsome, and loved by all. He was always successful. Everyone knew that he would someday become king.

In a nearby kingdom, the good King Janaka had a beautiful daughter, Sita. She was born with the spirit of Vishnu's wife, the goddess Lakshmi. She was graceful, with long, flowing hair. She, too, was loved by everyone.

Sita's father wanted only the best man to marry his daughter, so he tested those who hoped to win her hand. Rama succeeded,

The wedding of Rama and Sita is depicted, or shown, in artwork throughout Indian history.

and he and Sita had a grand wedding and happily began their life together.

Rama had a beautiful wife and was set to be the next leader of his kingdom, but Rama's stepmother wanted her son, Bharat, to be king. She asked the king to send Rama away. The king had once promised his wife that he would grant her two wishes, so he told Rama to leave the kingdom. He granted her wish, even though it hurt his son.

DANGER IN THE FOREST

Rama's brother, Lakshmana, went with Rama and Sita to live in the forest. The forest was filled with many wild beasts and evil spirits. Rama and Lakshmana fought many of them and always won.

However, the two brothers found a strong enemy in the king of demons, or evil spirits, known as Ravana. It's been said that he had 10 heads and 20 arms and was very powerful. Ravana kidnapped Sita, taking her from her husband and his brother.

Rama and Lakshmana wandered through the forest looking for Sita. Along the way, they met an army of magical monkeys. With the monkeys' help, they planned to find and attack Ravana's kingdom—Lanka.

LIGHTING THE WAY

Rama eventually reached Lanka and fought Ravana to free Sita. Rama killed Ravana in the battle. Sita was freed and was reunited with her husband.

This wasn't the only happy reunion. After 14 years away from home, Rama was allowed to come back to Ayodhya. He and Sita would rule as king and queen.

There was a grand celebration for King Rama and Queen Sita. The royal families ordered that the cities and kingdoms be lit

The lights that are lit for Diwali symbolize the lights that lit Rama and Sita's way home.

with rows of shining lamps to light their way home. The lights provided a warm welcome back after so many years of struggling in the forest.

Today, during the festival of Diwali, thousands of small lamps are lit just as they were for Rama and Sita's return. This festival of light celebrates the hope that—just as Rama was able to defeat the demon king—good will always win over evil.

EPIC POEMS

Ramayana is an epic poem. This means it's a long poem that tells a story. Epic poems often feature exciting tales of heroes and gods, such as Rama. These heroes often go on long journeys and have to face many obstacles, or things that get in the way of what they want. For example, Rama had to wander in the forest for 14 years and fight a demon king before he could save his wife and return home. This style of poetry was also popular in ancient Greece and Rome.

Although other groups also celebrate Diwali for different reasons, it's known mainly as a Hindu holiday and is celebrated by Hindu families around the world.

CHAPTER THREE

A Hindu Holiday

The story of Rama is connected to the Hindu religion. This ancient belief system is still practiced by around 1 billion people who live in many different countries, although India is the center of the global Hindu community. For these people, Diwali is a celebration of their beliefs, so understanding the basic beliefs of Hinduism is an important part of understanding Diwali.

Basic Beliefs

Hindus worship different gods and goddesses, but many also believe in a kind of spirit called *brahman* that is in all things all the time. It's known as the spirit behind all change in the universe and is eternal, or never-ending. Different groups of Hindus have different ideas about brahman, but the belief in its central **role** as the absolute truth and **reality** in the world is shared by most Hindus.

Hindus also believe that every person has a soul or a true self, called atman. Hinduism teaches that when a person dies, their soul can be born again as another person or another living thing. This is called reincarnation. How a person is reborn in

Many people who follow Hinduism have one god or goddess they pray to more often than others.

Karma and Castes

Most Hindus believe that a person's karma—the force created by the good and bad deeds they've done on Earth—**determines** their place in this life and the next. This belief is at the center of a social system in India known as the caste system. Different groups of people are ranked in society—with priests and teachers at the top and laborers at the bottom. Some people believe that those in a lower caste ended up there because they did bad things in a past life. This led to discrimination, or unfair and unkind treatment, toward the lower castes in Indian society. Although India legally got rid of the caste system in 1950, people still follow it today.

the next life depends on how they live in their present life. You can be born into a better life if you do more good actions than bad actions. The force behind this is known as karma. Many Hindus also believe that there is an end to this cycle when a person's soul is set free.

People in different parts of India and around the world practice Hinduism in many ways. Hindus believe in many gods and often favor one god over others. However, they view all the gods as different ways brahman is **expressed**. For example, the three main gods in Hinduism are Brahman or Brahma (the god of creation), Vishnu (the god in charge of protecting the world), and Shiva (the god of **destruction**).

How Hindus Worship

Hindus worship, or honor, their gods in a way that's known as puja. Formal worship takes place in a temple, or holy building. However,

Holidays such as Diwali are an important time for Hindu families to talk about their beliefs and to share special traditions.

Hindus also often have a shrine, or an area for worship, at home. These shrines are often focused on certain gods and goddesses that a family sees as important or especially helpful. Puja plays an important part in celebrations of Diwali.

Like many religions around the world, Hinduism has its own holy texts, or written works. These are collected in works known as the Vedas, which were written in Sanskrit around 1500 BCE.

MANY DIFFERENT FORMS

Like most major religions, Hinduism has many different branches. Different families honor different gods in their homes. In addition, different groups have different beliefs about the gods, the best ways to live, and other important aspects, or parts, of this religion. For example, some Hindus are vegetarians, which means they don't eat meat. This is because they believe all life is sacred, or holy. However, others enjoy some kinds of meat and only stay away from anything that comes from a cow—the most sacred animal in the Hindu religion.

With more than 1 billion people practicing Hinduism around the world, the **rituals** and traditions that go along with this religion will often look different from place to place—and from family to family. This includes Diwali traditions.

Diwali is a special time for Hindu families, and special times often call for special clothes. Buying a new outfit is just one way people prepare for this holiday.

CHAPTER FOUR
Getting Ready

Hindu families sometimes follow a different calendar than the one followed by most people in the United States. The months have different names, and Diwali happens in the month of Kartika. In the United States, the date of Diwali changes every year.

Even if the exact date may change from year to year, many Diwali traditions stay the same and have for a long time. These traditions often begin with preparing the home for the holiday.

Looking Nice

Families around the world have a lot to do to prepare for Diwali. They usually begin by making their homes very clean. Hindus believe the goddess Lakshmi only brings wealth and good fortune to very clean homes.

Many families buy new clothes for Diwali. Some people choose to wear traditional Indian clothes. Women and girls may choose to wear saris. These are pieces of colorful cloth that are wrapped around the body. Men and boys may wear loose-fitting shirts called kurtas over pants. Many Hindus take great pride in their traditional clothing, especially for holidays such as Diwali. However, others dress up in dresses, pants, and shirts that are less traditional and more like the clothing worn by most Americans or other people in Western countries.

People do not only shop for new clothes for Diwali. They also like to buy and wear new gold jewelry. In fact, the first day of Diwali—Dhanteras—is known as the day to buy gold, silver, and other fancy things. This holiday starts in style!

Favorite Foods

After cleaning the house and getting dressed up, it's time to eat. People love to eat sweet treats and delicious foods during Diwali. *Rasgullas* are milk dumplings dipped in syrup. *Jalebi* is a treat that looks like a twisted pretzel. It's made from a flour batter that's fried. Like rasgullas, it's also dipped in sugary syrup. *Barfi* is a fudge treat made with milk, sugar, nuts, flour, fruits, and sometimes even vegetables!

There are more than 100 different ways to wear a sari!

Indians often enjoy drinking lassi. It's made with yogurt, fruit, and spices. Mango lassi is popular because mangoes are grown in India.

Sweets are a big part of Diwali, but they're not the whole meal. Traditional Indian dishes are served throughout the holiday. Curry is a common part of Indian cooking. It's a mixture of spices used to flavor chicken, vegetables, and other foods. These foods are often eaten with rice and a flat bread called chapati. Samosas are little pastries that are often filled with potatoes before being deep-fried. They're a popular Indian snack at any time of year, including Diwali.

Sending Cards

Just as cards have become an important part of Christmas, many people like to send each other Diwali cards. The cards may have pictures of the goddess Lakshmi or the god Ganesh (or Ganesha). Ganesh is usually shown with the head of an elephant.

Shown here is a plate filled with Diwali treats.

Hindu people pray to Ganesh before starting something new. Because many Indians see Diwali as the start of a new year, this god is an important part of the holiday.

Sending cards to family and friends is one way to spread the joyful spirit of Diwali. It's a time to celebrate light, and cards can often brighten someone's day.

Diwali Gifts

Another way people prepare for Diwali is by buying gifts for their family members and friends. Giving gifts is an important part of this holiday because it spreads joy and brings people together. It's also a way to show someone you wish good things for them in the coming year. Diwali gifts can be traditional, such as saris, or more modern, such as the latest toys or most expensive jewelry.

Lights and bright colors are an important part of Diwali celebrations around the world.

CHAPTER FIVE

The Days of Diwali

Preparing for Diwali isn't easy—foods need to be made, saris need to be wrapped, and gifts and cards need to be bought. However, once the work is done, it's time to celebrate! Each day of Diwali has different traditions with special meanings behind them.

Decorations and Diyas

The first day of Diwali is often seen as a day of preparation. It's the day to buy gold, clean the house, and decorate. Hindus decorate doorways to homes, shops, temples, and restaurants for Diwali with colorful **designs** called *rangoli*. This is a very old art form that uses colored powder to form patterns, pictures, and words on the ground. Pictures of flowers, animals, gods, goddesses, temples, and oil lamps are common rangoli designs. Sometimes, small footprints are drawn to welcome Lakshmi.

Early on the second day, people take a bath with special oils and **herbs**. Everyone dresses in new or newly washed clothes, and lights are placed around the house. A *diya* is a traditional

Rangoli can be seen around homes, business, and public places in India during Diwali and other important celebrations.

A New Beginning for Businesses

Diwali is a time to start fresh, and Hindu business owners do this by closing their accounts from the past year and paying back money that they owe. Then, they perform a ritual called *chopda pujan* to bring good luck to their businesses before they open their accounts for the new year.

oil lamp made from baked clay. Before people had electric lights, they used diyas on Diwali. The first diya would be lit, and it would be used to light all the others in the house. Some people still use diyas, but candles, electric lights, or handmade **lanterns** are more common today. Some houses light paths with candles to welcome Lakshmi, and other people set off fireworks to bring more light to the celebrations.

The Celebrations Continue

The third day of Diwali is when Lakshmi Puja is performed. This is a ritual to honor Lakshmi. Pujas can be performed at Hindu temples and at home. For Lakshmi Puja, people say prayers, light candles and other lights, and sing songs. Food and flowers are offered to Lakshmi. Then, people share big meals, exchange gifts, and set off more fireworks. It's believed that the loud noises of the fireworks keep evil away.

Families and friends get together during Diwali, and this is especially true for the last two days. In fact, the final day of Diwali is set aside for married women to invite their brothers to their home for a big meal. Diwali is a time for joy, and like most holidays around the world, people want to share that joy with their loved ones.

Lighting the Way

During Diwali, many parts of India glow with the light of oil lamps, candles, and electric lights. This beautiful sight reminds people to find the lights in the darkness—and to be lights to others. This hopeful message is one that Hindus carry with them into a new year.

Many **cultures** around the world gather together to celebrate the light. Even though the celebrations might look different and the names aren't the same, they're all connected by the idea of hope that's at the center of Diwali. This special day brightens the path to a new year for more than a billion people around the world, and that is certainly something to celebrate.

Celebrating Diwali connects Hindus around the world to their past and to each other.

HOLIDAY HOW-TO

Make Your Own Rangoli Decoration

You Will Need:

1 paper plate

colored craft paper or construction paper in five to six different colors

pencil

scissors

glue

This is an example of the kind of rangoli pattern you can make on your paper plate.

Directions:

1. Choose one color of paper for each shape on your decoration. Draw the shapes on the papers, and cut them out with the scissors. Examples of shapes include triangles, squares, rectangles, teardrops, diamonds, and half circles.

2. Cut one circle shape, and glue it in the center of the paper plate.

3. Glue the other shapes in rings around the center circle. For example, the triangles can be the next ring, and the squares can come after that. Keep making rings until you've used all your shapes.

4. Cut the edges of the paper plate to give it a zigzag border.

GLOSSARY

culture: The beliefs and ways of life of a certain group of people.

design: A decorative pattern.

destruction: Causing so much harm to something that it can't be fixed.

determine: To officially decide something.

express: To make known.

herb: A low-growing plant used to make medicine or give food flavor.

lantern: A light that usually has a glass covering and can be carried by a handle.

reality: The way things actually are.

ritual: A religious ceremony, especially one consisting of a series of actions performed in a certain order.

role: A part or function.

symbolize: To stand for something else.

tradition: A way of thinking, behaving, or doing something that's been used by people in a particular society for a long time.

FIND OUT MORE

BOOKS

Quinlan, Julia J. *Hinduism*. New York, NY: Britannica Educational Publishing, 2019.

Senker, Cath. *A Hindu Life*. New York, NY: PowerKids Press, 2020.

Vallepur, Shalini. *Diwali*. King's Lynn, UK: BookLife Publishing, 2020.

WEBSITES

All About Diwali—The Festival of Lights!
www.cbc.ca/kidscbc2/the-feed/whats-the-story-diwali
This website features facts about Diwali and descriptions of how it's celebrated in different parts of the world—from India to Canada.

"Diwali: Festival of Lights"
kids.nationalgeographic.com/pages/article/Diwali
This *National Geographic Kids* article breaks down the days of Diwali and includes beautiful pictures of Diwali celebrations.

Publisher's note to educators and parents: Our editors have carefully reviewed these websites to ensure that they are suitable for students. Many websites change frequently, however, and we cannot guarantee that a site's future contents will continue to meet our high standards of quality and educational value. Be advised that students should be closely supervised whenever they access the Internet.

INDEX